Eerie Inns

by Natalie Lunis

Consultant: Troy Taylor
President of the American Ghost Society

BEARPORT
PUBLISHING

New York, New York

Credits

Cover and Title Page, © ysbrandcosijn/fotolia.com, © Christian Delber/fotolia.com, © Vasina Nazarenko/fotolia.com, and © Eric Isselée/fotolia.com; 4–5, © Kim Jones; 6, © Susan Cole Kelly; 6BL, © Allie Richards; 7, © Culture Club/Getty Images; 8, © Steve Dunwell; 9T, © PoodlesRock/Corbis; 9B, © John P Kelly; 10BR, © Hoffman Photography; 10, © Andre Jenny/Alamy; 11T, © The Granger Collection, NYC; 11B, © Chamille White/iStockphoto; 12T, © De Agostini/G. Dagli Orti/The Granger Collection; 12B, © Diane Stoneback/MCT/Landov; 13, © NULL/Alamy; 14R, © F1online digitale Bildagentur GmbH/Alamy; 14TL, © Danita Delimont/Alamy; 15T, © North Wind Picture Archives/North Wind; 15B, © Danita Delimont/Alamy; 16, © pf/Alamy; 17, © Courtesy of Queen Anne Hotel; 18, © Lauren Zeid/eStock Photo; 19, © Wikipedia; 20, © Bruce Hunt Images; 21, © Burke/Triolo Productions; 22, © Billy Hathorn/Wikipedia; 23, © David Sucsy; 24, © Ozzy Delaney; 25T, © The Granger Collection, New York/The Granger Collection; 25B, © Courtesy of The Talbot Hotel, Oundle, Northamptonshire; 26, © Photograph taken by Leo Meyer; 27, © akg-images/ullstein bild; 31, © iStockphoto/Thinkstock.

Publisher: Kenn Goin
Editorial Director: Adam Siegel
Creative Director: Spencer Brinker
Design: Dawn Beard Creative
Cover: Kim Jones
Photo Researcher: Picture Perfect Professionals, LLC

Library of Congress Cataloging-in-Publication Data in process at time of publication (2014)
Library of Congress Control Number: 2013039375
ISBN-13: 978-1-62724-090-1 (library binding)

For more information, write to Bearport Publishing Company, Inc., 45 West 21st Street, Suite 3B, New York, New York 10010. Printed in the United States of America.

10 9 8 7 6 5 4 3 2 1

Contents

Eerie Inns

For most travelers, an inn is a small, comfortable place to get a bite to eat and rest for a while before continuing on a journey. An inn can also be a place to spend a few nights while taking in the sights of a charming town. What happens, however, if some of the guests at one of these small hotels refuse to check out? What if their ghosts have decided to stay forever?

Within the 11 **eerie** inns in this book, you will meet several **spirits**, including a ghost who likes to tap-dance, a teacher who can't stop tidying up after others, and a queen who is still walking down a stairway to her death. Don't stay around them too long, however. They might keep you from getting a good night's sleep!

Portrait of a Ghost

Longfellow's Wayside Inn, Sudbury, Massachusetts

Longfellow's Wayside Inn is the oldest inn in America that is still open to guests. It was started in 1716 by David Howe and his wife, Hepzibah. Other members of the family ran the business until 1861. One of them, it seems, never left—even long after new owners took over.

WELCOME TO
Longfellow's
WAYSIDE INN
· A NATIONAL HISTORIC SITE ·

Jerusha Howe was the great-granddaughter of the inn's first owners. Lively and talented, she was known for playing the piano for guests. Sometime in the early 1800s, she fell in love with an Englishman. He was sailing back to England soon, but he promised to return and marry her. Sadly, he was never heard from again. Jerusha was heartbroken. After his disappearance, she rarely left her room on the second floor until her death in 1842.

Since then, people claim that Jerusha has reappeared as a ghost—mostly on the second floor. There, guests have reported hearing unexplained footsteps, soft piano music, and noticed the smell of a lemony perfume. Some visitors—mostly male ones—have felt a spirit touch them as they walked by. Others have heard whisperings in their ears.

One female guest actually saw the inn's ghost so clearly that she was able to draw her. Did the picture look just like the woman who had lived on the second floor more than 100 years ago? No one knows, because no drawings were made of Jerusha during her lifetime.

The inn is named for the famous American poet Henry Wadsworth Longfellow. After staying at the inn in 1862, Longfellow wrote a book of stories, called *Tales of a Wayside Inn*, based on his visit. After the book was published, the inn's owner changed its name from Howe's Tavern to Longfellow's Wayside Inn.

Henry Wadsworth Longfellow
(1807–1882)

Home at Last

Jared Coffin House, Nantucket, Massachusetts

With its history of **seafaring** and **whaling**, it's no wonder that the Massachusetts island of Nantucket is said to be filled with ghosts. After all, many young sailors lost their lives while at sea. One Nantucket sea captain, however, followed a different course. He lived a long life before coming back to haunt the house that he had built on the island.

Jared Coffin House

Jared Coffin was not only a sea captain but also a successful owner of whaling ships. As a result, in 1845, he was able to have a three-story brick **mansion** built for himself and his wife in the center of Nantucket. Within less than a year, however, the Coffins went off to live in Boston. Why? Some people say that Mrs. Coffin wanted to live in a big city. Others say that she disliked the smell of whale **blubber** as it was being melted down in a nearby building to make lamp oil and other products.

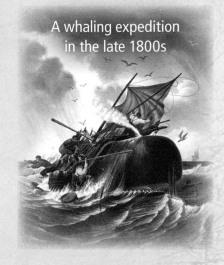

A whaling expedition in the late 1800s

About a year after its owners left, the house survived a fire that burned down much of the town around it. The building was then bought and turned into an inn. According to those who know the place well, guests are not the only ones who enjoy its comforts. Often, when there is an empty rocking chair near a cozy fire, it rocks slowly back and forth. People say it isn't really empty, however. Instead, it's occupied by the spirit of Jared Coffin—back to enjoy his beautiful Nantucket home at last.

The Jared Coffin House survived the fire of 1846 because it was made of brick. The houses and buildings that burned were made of wood.

Tap . . . Tap . . . Tap

The Green Mountain Inn, Stowe, Vermont

Often, when ghosts are present in a home or an inn, it's because they are the spirits of people who were born or died there. Or perhaps they spent an especially important part of their lives in the building. All of these facts are true in the case of Boots Berry, whose ghost has haunted a Vermont inn since the 1800s.

The Green Mountain Inn

Boots Berry lived a life that was full of ups and downs. In 1840, the year he was born, his mother worked as a maid at the Green Mountain Inn, and his father worked as a **horseman**. Boots grew up at the inn, and, in time, he became a horseman as well. He also became a hometown hero one day when he stopped the horses pulling a runaway **stagecoach** and saved the lives of the passengers inside.

Horsemen at work

Sadly, the Vermont man's life took a downward turn after that. He started drinking too much and was fired from his job. He then wandered near and far, ending up in jail in New Orleans. It was there that he got his nickname, Boots, when a fellow prisoner taught him to tap-dance.

After a while, Boots returned to Vermont and the inn. There, he again saved a life when a little girl became trapped on the roof during a snowstorm. Boots helped her back to safety, but then slipped and fell off the roof to his death. Since that time, on cold, stormy nights, people inside the inn say they have heard the sound of tapping coming from the top of the building.

Boots was born on the inn's third floor in Room 302. People say that when he slipped off the roof, he fell past the window of this room. Today, Room 302 is where Boots's tapping can be heard the loudest.

Ghosts of Gettysburg

Farnsworth House Inn, Gettysburg, Pennsylvania

Guests at this Pennsylvania inn claim that the ghost of a boy who plays tricks appears in one of the rooms. The spirit of a man who is thought to be his father has been heard pacing nervously in the hall outside. That's only a small part of the ghostly activity at this inn, however. After all, the building is located in the heart of Gettysburg—a place where thousands died in one of the bloodiest battles of the **Civil War**.

Farnsworth House Inn

A painting of the Battle of Gettysburg

The 200-year-old building now known as the Farnsworth House Inn started taking in paying guests around 1900. Not long after, people say, a terrible accident occurred there. A young boy ran out into the street and was hit by a horse-drawn carriage. He was brought indoors and a doctor was called, but it was too late. The boy died while his father waited and worried. Today, some people believe that both the young boy and his father have remained at the inn as ghosts.

Their spirits are far from alone, however. About forty years before the boy's death, from July 1 to July 3, 1863, around 165,000 Civil War soldiers from the North and South fought each other in and around Gettysburg. During the three-day battle, a group of Southern **sharpshooters** entered the building, which was still a private home at the time. They stationed themselves at windows in the attic and in other rooms. By the end of the three days, the sharpshooters were killed, along with about 7,000 other soldiers on both sides. The presence of the Southern soldiers is still sensed by visitors to the Farnsworth House Inn, especially in the form of voices and footsteps—all coming from the attic.

Today, much of Gettysburg is said to be haunted by the spirits of Civil War soldiers who died there. Many people say that a fog—with horses and riders moving inside it—sometimes appears on the former battlefield at night.

One Last Leap

La Fonda on the Plaza, Santa Fe, New Mexico

The hotel that now stands on the **Plaza** in Santa Fe has been around since 1922. However, there has been some kind of inn or hotel there for 400 years, going all the way back to the days when New Mexico was a Spanish **colony**. Since then, many ghosts are said to have gathered at the busy spot in the center of town—including one who can't stop repeating his last day on Earth.

La Fonda on the Plaza

During the 1800s, Santa Fe's downtown area—and its hotel—became busier than ever. That's because in 1821, the Santa Fe Trail was opened. The 900-mile-long (1,448 km) **route** connected the capital of New Mexico to Franklin, Missouri. It provided a path for **pioneers**, cowboys, and traders through the American West.

Santa Fe in the 1800s

By the 1860s, thousands of people were traveling and doing business along the Trail. One of them was a salesman who stopped at Santa Fe's Plaza and spent time at a popular **gambling hall** that belonged to the hotel. Not being very lucky, however, the man lost all his company's money. As soon as he realized what he had done, he jumped to his death down a deep **well** that was just outside the hall.

The restaurant at today's La Fonda on the Plaza is built over the spot where that well once stood. According to diners and staff members, the ghost of the salesman, dressed in the clothing of the 1800s, sometimes makes a shocking appearance. Even more shocking is the way the ghost disappears—by jumping into the floor and the unseen well that lies beneath.

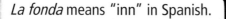

La fonda means "inn" in Spanish.

La Fonda's restaurant

15

A Ghostly Welcome

The Queen Anne Hotel, San Francisco, California

The building that now serves as the Queen Anne Hotel was not always a place for travelers and other overnight guests to stay. When it was built in 1890, it served as Miss Mary Lake's School for Girls. Mary Lake, the **headmistress**, showed great kindness and helpfulness as a teacher. Many people think she continues to show these qualities as she haunts the place she once loved.

The Queen Anne Hotel

Unfortunately, Miss Mary Lake's School closed after only six years—probably because there was not enough money to keep the expensive girls' **boarding school** running. For the next forty years, the elegant pink building that had housed the school was used by different groups. Then, for the next fifty, it mostly stood empty and run-down. Finally, during the 1980s, it was restored—inside and out—to its former beauty and reopened as the Queen Anne Hotel.

Many guests and workers who have spent time there believe that the hotel's appearance is not the only thing that goes back to the building's early days. They're also convinced that Mary Lake has returned to the inn's rooms and hallways. What makes them think so? Mary's reflection has often been seen in a hall mirror. In addition, a misty figure is sometimes spotted in the hall. Even more mysteriously, in certain rooms, bags have been unpacked and clothing has been hung up when no one was around. One guest was even tucked in during a nap. It seems that after a long time of being away, Mary is happy to once again show her caring nature.

Inside the Queen Anne Hotel

People say that Mary is most active in Suite 410—a room with a fireplace and an extra sitting area that was once her office at the school.

Robert the Doll

The Artist House, Key West, Florida

Many inns and small hotels were once private homes. That's true of the Artist House. The beautiful Florida mansion was once the home of a famous painter. It was also the home of a very strange doll named Robert, who seems to have had a mind of its own.

The Artist House

The inn now known as the Artist House was built in the late 1890s by Thomas Otto and his wife, Minnie. In 1898, their four-year-old son, Robert Eugene Otto, received a cloth doll as a gift. The doll looked like a life-size boy and wore a sailor suit. Its young owner, who was known as "Gene," gave it his own first name, Robert.

Before long, people started noticing strange things about Robert, such as changes in the doll's expression. Children on the street said they saw the doll move while it sat by an attic window. Sometimes the sound of giggling came from the top floor when Robert was up there alone.

During the 1920s, Gene left home to study painting in New York and Paris. Then, he returned to the house where he had grown up, bringing his new wife, Anne, with him. According to reports, the couple found Robert there, and the strange events began occurring all over again. After Gene's death, the house became a hotel. What happened to Robert? By that time he was famous in Key West, and so he was given to a small museum in town. Reportedly, he continues to cause **mischief** there.

Robert the Doll

It is said that visitors to the museum must ask Robert's permission before taking a photo—otherwise the doll will put a **curse** on them and bring them bad luck. The walls of the glass case where Robert is kept are covered with letters asking him to remove some of these curses.

The Lady with the Lantern

Casablanca Inn, St. Augustine, Florida

St. Augustine, Florida, is the oldest city in the United States. It also has the country's oldest **port**. As a result of its long history and seaside location, many stories from its past are filled with pirates and **smugglers**. One of the eeriest tells of a ghost that is still sending secret messages to ships from one waterfront inn.

Casablanca Inn

Casablanca Inn was built in 1914 on an old street with a good view of the water. During the 1920s, a local **widow** bought it and gave it its current name. At first, the inn was a success, always clean and comfortable and filled with guests. After a while, however, its owner needed more money to keep the inn running. It was then that she started doing business with rum-runners.

Alcohol, including rum, was illegal during this period of American history, known as **Prohibition**. Rum-runners—people who transported and sold rum—needed to steer clear of government agents. To help them do so, the owner of the Casablanca Inn would send a warning if she knew the agents were in town by climbing to the roof of the inn and swinging a lantern. If the smugglers, who were traveling in boats, saw the light, they would keep going. Today, almost one hundred years later, people in boats off the coast as well as visitors walking along the waterfront sometimes see a light swinging in the same spot—even though no one is there.

People in St. Augustine know the innkeeper's name but they usually call her simply the Lady with the Lantern. They keep her real name private out of respect for the rest of her family, because what she did was illegal.

Remember the Alamo!

The Menger Hotel, San Antonio, Texas

Over time, the Menger Hotel has become known not only as one of the finest places to stay in Texas but also one of the most haunted. Some of its ghosts are found within the historic building on Alamo Square. Others roam just outside.

MENGER HOTEL.

When it was first built in 1859, the Menger Hotel was no more than a small inn. Tired cowboys spent the night there before moving on. The place was so successful, however, that its owner, William Menger, soon added on another building. Then more rooms were built. By the end of the 1800s, the Menger was drawing people not only from all over Texas, but from all over the world. Presidents Ulysses S. Grant and Theodore Roosevelt are a few of the famous people who have stayed there.

According to some guests, the hotel has drawn many ghosts as well. Among those who have been spotted inside are Sallie White, a hotel maid who was murdered by her husband in 1876, and Richard King, a wealthy rancher who died in one of the rooms in 1885. Just outside the hotel is the Alamo—once a Spanish **mission**, then a **fort** where around 200 Texans died while fighting for independence from Mexico in 1836. Guests whose windows look out onto the Alamo claimed to have seen ghosts of the battle wandering the grounds at night.

After the battle of the Alamo, the general in charge of the Mexican troops ordered his men to destroy the fort. According to **legend**, however, when the men started to tear down the fort's walls, ghostly hands reached out to stop them. The terrified men fled, and the Alamo remained standing.

The Alamo

Stairway to Death

The Talbot Hotel, Oundle, England

More than 400 years ago, Mary, Queen of Scots was **executed** by her enemies in an English castle. Yet today she has been seen—in the form of a ghost—walking to her death down a stairway in a hotel that is about three and a half miles (5.6 km) away. Why is she there?

The Talbot Hotel

In 1586, Mary Stuart—also known as Mary, Queen of Scots—was put on trial for plotting against her cousin Elizabeth, who was Queen of England. Mary was found guilty, and not long after, she was sentenced to be **beheaded**. Both the trial and the execution took place at Fotheringhay Castle in the central part of England.

Mary, Queen of Scots
(1542–1587)

About fifty years after Mary's death, the castle was abandoned and **demolished**. However, people from nearby towns took away the materials that had been used to build it. Stones from its walls as well as windows and a beautiful oak staircase were used to rebuild a very old **tavern** in the town of Oundle.

Today, that English tavern is a hotel with 35 rooms, known as the Talbot. Guests and workers there sometimes see a ghostly woman in a long dress on the staircase. Sometimes she is gazing out the window at the top of the staircase. Other times, she starts coming down the stairs. Not surprisingly, people assume the ghost is Mary, retracing the steps she walked on the last day of her life.

People in the hotel have also heard sobbing coming from one of the rooms. However, when they checked, there was no one inside.

The oak staircase at the Talbot Hotel

A Real Murder Mystery

The Savoy Hotel, Mussoorie, India

High up in the Himalaya Mountains, the Savoy Hotel has long been a place for people to enjoy spectacular views and breathe fresh mountain air. Over the years, all kinds of interesting people, including members of royalty, politicians, and writers from many different countries, have stayed there. The popular mountainside **resort** was not always peaceful and restful, however. At one time, it was the setting for a murder.

The Savoy Hotel

In 1911, the Savoy Hotel was at the height of its popularity. Among the stylish guests that it attracted were Frances Garnett-Orme and her friend Eva Mountstephen. Both women were from England and had lived and traveled widely in India.

Tragically, their stay at the hotel ended in death. One morning, Frances was found dead in her room. The doctor who examined her body determined that she had been poisoned. Eva, who had left the hotel a few days earlier, was arrested and accused of poisoning Frances, but she was never found guilty of the crime. Neither was anyone else.

Since the unsolved murder, guests have reported seeing a female ghost wandering the halls and staring ahead with a strange expression. She is thought to be Frances, still looking for the person who caused her death.

Agatha Christie
(1890–1976)

Mystery writer Agatha Christie read about the murder case and used some of the details for the plot of her first novel, *The Mysterious Affair at Styles*. Christie's story is not set at an Indian hotel, however. Instead, it takes place at an English country house.

Eerie Inns

The Green Mountain Inn
Stowe, Vermont
The sound of a tap-dancing ghost is heard on the roof.

Longfellow's Wayside Inn
Sudbury, Massachusetts
A spirit waits for a traveler's return.

The Queen Anne Hotel
San Francisco, California
A schoolteacher welcomes guests—just as she once welcomed new pupils when she was alive.

NORTH AMERICA

Atlantic Ocean

Jared Coffin House
Nantucket, Massachusetts
A sea captain's ghost enjoys a well-earned rest.

La Fonda on the Plaza
Santa Fe, New Mexico
A gambler loses everything— including his life.

Pacific Ocean

SOUTH AMERICA

Farnsworth House Inn
Gettysburg, Pennsylvania
An accident and a bloody battle both leave behind ghosts.

The Menger Hotel
San Antonio, Texas
Just outside this hotel, ghosts relive a battle for independence.

The Artist House
Key West, Florida
A small hotel was once the home of a haunted doll.

Casablanca Inn
St. Augustine, Florida
An innkeeper continues to signal to smugglers.

Around the World

The Talbot Hotel
Oundle, England

A queen appears on a staircase—on her way to her execution.

EUROPE

ASIA

AFRICA

The Savoy Hotel
Mussoorie, India

A ghost searches for the person who poisoned her.

Arctic Ocean

Indian Ocean

AUSTRALIA

Southern Ocean

ANTARCTICA

Glossary

beheaded (bi-HED-id) put to death by having one's head chopped off

blubber (BLUH-bur) a layer of fat under the skin of whales

boarding school (BORD-ing SKOOL) a school where students live and study

Civil War (SIV-il WOR) the U.S. war between the Southern states and the Northern states, which lasted from 1861 to 1865

colony (KOL-uh-nee) an area that has been settled by people from another country and is ruled by that country

curse (KURSS) something that brings or causes evil or misfortune

demolished (di-MOL-ished) destroyed

eerie (EER-ee) mysterious, strange

executed (EK-suh-*kyoo*-tid) put to death

fort (FORT) a strong building from which people can defend an area

gambling hall (GAM-bling HALL) a place where people play cards and other games of chance to win money

headmistress (HED-*miss*-truhss) a female teacher who is in charge of a school

horseman (HORSS-muhn) a person who takes care of horses

legend (LEJ-uhnd) a story handed down from the past that may be based on fact but is not always completely true

mansion (MAN-shuhn) a very large and grand house

mischief (MISS-chif) playful behavior that may cause trouble

mission (MISH-uhn) a place where a religious group teaches and does community work

pioneers (*pye*-uh-NEERZ) people who go to live in a place that has not yet been settled

plaza (PLAH-zuh) a town square

port (PORT) a place where ships load and unload goods

Prohibition (proh-uh-BISH-uhn) the period of time in U.S. history, between 1920 and 1933, when the sale of alcohol was against the law

resort (ri-ZORT) a place where tourists relax and have fun

route (ROOT) the road a person follows to get from one place to another

seafaring (SEE-*fair*-ing) going, traveling, or working on the sea

sharpshooters (SHARP-*shoo*-turz) soldiers who fire on an enemy from a hidden spot as well as from a distance

smugglers (SMUHG-lurz) people who secretly bring in or take out goods in a way that is against the law

spirits (SPIHR-its) supernatural creatures, such as ghosts

stagecoach (STAYJ-kohch) a carriage that is pulled by horses

tavern (TAV-urn) a place where people stop to eat and drink

well (WEL) a deep hole dug in the ground to get water

whaling (HWAY-ling) the hunting of whales from ships at sea

widow (WID-oh) a woman whose husband has died

Bibliography

Austin, Joanne. *Weird Hauntings: True Tales of Ghostly Places.* New York: Sterling (2006).

Hauck, Dennis William. *Haunted Places: The National Directory: Ghostly Abodes, Sacred Sites, UFO Landings, and Other Supernatural Locations.* New York: Penguin Books (2002).

Jasper, Mark. *Haunted Inns of New England.* Yarmouth Port, MA: On Cape Publications (2000).

Smith, Terry L., and Mark Jean. *Haunted Inns of America: National Directory of Haunted Hotels and Bed & Breakfast Inns.* Birmingham, AL: Crane Hill (2003).

Read More

Hamilton, John. *Haunted Places (The World of Horror).* Edina, MN: ABDO (2007).

Parvis, Sarah. *Haunted Hotels (Scary Places).* New York: Bearport (2008).

Williams, Dinah. *Haunted Houses (Scary Places).* New York: Bearport (2008).

Wood, Ted. *Ghosts of the Southwest: The Phantom Gunslinger and Other Real-Life Hauntings.* New York: Walker (1997).

Learn More Online

To learn more about eerie inns, visit
www.bearportpublishing.com/ScaryPlaces

Index

About the Author

Natalie Lunis has written many nonfiction books for children.
She lives in New York's lower Hudson River Valley—the home
of the Headless Horseman.